Cheesecake Pudding Cookbook

Delicious collection of creamy cheesecake pudding recipes

CHEESECAKE PUDDING COOKBOOK

First edition. November 1, 2023.

ISBN: 979-8223350125

Written by john ahmad.

Table of Contents

Cheesecake Pudding Cookbook 1

Chapter 1: Introduction to Cheesecake Pudding | Section 1.1: The Irresistible Charm of Cheesecake Pudding 2

Section 1.2: A Brief History of Cheesecake and Pudding 3

Section 1.3: The Marriage of Two Classics 4

Section 1.4: Ingredients and Equipment 5

Chapter 2: The Basics of Cheesecake Pudding | Section 2.1: Understanding the Elements of Cheesecake Pudding 7

Section 2.2: Selecting the Perfect Cream Cheese 9

Section 2.3: The Role of Sweeteners in Cheesecake Pudding 10

Section 2.4: Achieving the Perfect Texture with Eggs 11

Section 2.5: Flavor Enhancements with Extracts and Flavorings.12

Section 2.6: Mastering the Mixing Techniques 13

Section 2.7: Baking and Cooling Techniques 14

Chapter 3: Classic Cheesecake Pudding Recipes | Section 3.1: Classic Vanilla Cheesecake Pudding 16

Section 3.2: Decadent Chocolate Cheesecake Pudding 18

Chapter 4: Fruity Bliss: Fruit-Infused Cheesecake Pudding | Section 4.1: Strawberry Cheesecake Pudding 20

Section 4.2: Tropical Mango Cheesecake Pudding 22

Chapter 5: Chocolate Lover's Paradise: Decadent Chocolate Cheesecake Pudding | Section 5.1: Dark Chocolate Cheesecake Pudding 24

Section 5.2: White Chocolate Raspberry Cheesecake Pudding ..26

Chapter 6: Nutty Twists: Nut-Infused Cheesecake Pudding Delights | Section 6.1: Hazelnut Praline Cheesecake Pudding............28

Section 6.2: Almond Joy Cheesecake Pudding 30

Chapter 7: Seasonal Sensations: Cheesecake Pudding for Every Season | Section 7.1: Springtime Lemon Cheesecake Pudding...........32

Section 7.2: Summertime Berry Cheesecake Pudding 34

Section 7.3: Autumn Spice Cheesecake Pudding 36

Section 7.4: Winter Wonderland Peppermint Cheesecake Pudding...38

Chapter 8: Exotic Variations: International Cheesecake Pudding Recipes | Section 8.1: Matcha Green Tea Cheesecake Pudding (Japan) 40

Section 8.2: Tiramisu Cheesecake Pudding (Italy) 42

Section 8.3: Coconut Pandan Cheesecake Pudding (Southeast Asia)...44

Chapter 9: No-Bake Cheesecake Pudding Recipes | Section 9.1: Cookies and Cream Cheesecake Pudding..46

Section 9.2: Peanut Butter Chocolate Cheesecake Pudding.........48

Section 9.3: Fresh Fruit Parfait Cheesecake Pudding.....................50

Chapter 10: Miniature Indulgences: Cheesecake Pudding for Single Servings | Section 10.1: Mini Strawberry Cheesecake Pudding Cups...52

Section 10.2: Mini Salted Caramel Cheesecake Pudding Jars 54

Section 10.3: Mini Chocolate Mint Cheesecake Pudding Jars.....56

Chapter 11: Holiday Extravaganza: Festive Cheesecake Pudding Creations | Section 11.1: Pumpkin Spice Cheesecake Pudding (Thanksgiving)...58

Section 11.2: Peppermint Bark Cheesecake Pudding (Christmas) 60

Section 11.3: Red, White, and Blue Cheesecake Pudding (Fourth of July)..62

Chapter 12: Cheesecake Pudding for Breakfast: Brunch-Inspired Delights | Section 12.1: Blueberry Almond Cheesecake Pudding Parfait 64

Section 12.2: Maple Walnut Cheesecake Pudding Bowl................66

Section 12.3: Raspberry Coconut Cheesecake Pudding Smoothie...67

Chapter 13: Light and Healthy: Guilt-Free Cheesecake Pudding Alternatives | Section 13.1: Greek Yogurt Cheesecake Pudding.........69

Section 13.2: Vegan Cheesecake Pudding with Cashews..............70

Section 13.3: Sugar-Free Cheesecake Pudding with Stevia 71

Chapter 14: Creamy Combinations: Cheesecake Pudding Pairings and Toppings | Section 14.1: Graham Cracker Crumble......................73

Section 14.2: Fresh Berry Compote 74

Section 14.3: Toasted Almond Slices 75

Chapter 15: Cheesecake Pudding for Kids: Fun and Wholesome Treats | Section 15.1: Mini Cheesecake Pudding Cups with Cookie Crust 76

Section 15.2: Cheesecake Pudding Parfait with Fresh Fruit 78

Section 15.3: Cheesecake Pudding Smoothie 79

Chapter 16: Gluten-Free and Vegan Cheesecake Pudding Recipes | Section 16.1: Almond Flour Crust Cheesecake Pudding Cups...........80

Section 16.2: Coconut Milk Cheesecake Pudding 82

Section 16.3: Cashew-Based Cheesecake Pudding 83

Chapter 17: Boozy and Bold: Cheesecake Pudding with Alcohol Infusions | Section 17.1: Baileys Irish Cream Cheesecake Pudding ...84

Section 17.2: Amaretto Infused Cheesecake Pudding 85

Section 17.3: Rum Raisin Cheesecake Pudding 86

Chapter 18: Chilled Delights: Cheesecake Pudding Frozen Desserts | Section 18.1: Cheesecake Pudding Ice Cream......................88

Section 18.2: Frozen Cheesecake Pudding Bars 90

Section 18.3: Cheesecake Pudding Popsicles 91

Chapter 19: Artful Presentation: Decorating and Garnishing Cheesecake Pudding | Section 19.1: Whipped Cream and Fresh Fruit Swirls...93

Section 19.2: Chocolate Ganache Drizzle 94

Section 19.3: Cookie Crumbs and Sprinkles 95

Section 19.4: Mint Leaves and Chocolate Shavings 96

Chapter 20: Cheesecake Pudding Masterclass: Advanced Techniques and Tips | Section 20.1: Achieving a Silky Smooth Texture...97

Section 20.2: Perfecting the Creaminess 98

Section 20.3: Preventing Cracking 99

Section 20.4: Experimenting with Flavors and Additions 100
Section 20.5: Serving and Storage Tips 101

John Ahmad

Chapter 1: Introduction to Cheesecake Pudding

Section 1.1: The Irresistible Charm of Cheesecake Pudding

Cheesecake Pudding possesses a unique and captivating allure that sets it apart from traditional cheesecakes or puddings. With its creamy, velvety texture and indulgent flavors, Cheesecake Pudding is a dessert sensation that captivates dessert enthusiasts worldwide. Prepare to be enchanted as we explore the irresistible charm of Cheesecake Pudding and discover why it has become a favorite treat among many.

Cheesecake Pudding entices with its smooth, luscious consistency that melts in your mouth with each spoonful. The combination of cream cheese, eggs, sugar, and other key ingredients creates a luxurious texture that is both creamy and light. It offers a delicate balance, where the richness of the cheesecake merges seamlessly with the silky smoothness of the pudding. The flavors are equally enchanting, ranging from classic vanilla to bold chocolate, tangy fruits, and delightful nut-infused variations. Whether enjoyed on its own or paired with complementary toppings, Cheesecake Pudding promises a delightful experience that satisfies even the most discerning sweet tooth.

Section 1.2: A Brief History of Cheesecake and Pudding

To truly appreciate the origins of Cheesecake Pudding, it is essential to understand the rich culinary heritage of its two main components: cheesecake and pudding. Cheesecake traces its roots back to ancient Greece, where it was served to athletes during the first Olympic Games. The Romans further refined cheesecake by introducing ingredients like honey and ricotta cheese, while medieval Europe developed variations using cream cheese.

Pudding, on the other hand, has a long history spanning various cultures and time periods. From ancient Egyptian rice and milk puddings to English custards and American-style puddings, the concept of thickened, sweetened mixtures has been enjoyed across civilizations. Puddings were often cherished for their comfort and versatility, making them suitable for both humble and extravagant occasions.

The combination of cheesecake and pudding is a natural progression, resulting in a dessert that captures the best of both worlds. It's a testament to the ingenuity of culinary enthusiasts who sought to enhance the creamy delight of cheesecake with the velvety smoothness of pudding. By merging these two beloved desserts, a new indulgence was born that would tantalize taste buds and become a delightful addition to dessert tables everywhere.

Section 1.3: The Marriage of Two Classics

Cheesecake Pudding represents a delightful fusion of flavors and textures, combining the velvety richness of cheesecake with the smooth and silky consistency of pudding. This section explores the artistry behind this marriage of two classics, highlighting how the unique characteristics of cheesecake and pudding complement each other to create a harmonious and indulgent dessert. The creamy and slightly tangy notes of cheesecake mingle with the silky, comforting embrace of pudding, resulting in a dessert that is truly greater than the sum of its parts.

Cheesecake Pudding offers a playfulness that traditional cheesecake or pudding alone cannot achieve. The creamy cheesecake layer adds depth and complexity, while the pudding layer contributes a delightful smoothness that envelops the palate. The contrasting textures and flavors create a symphony of taste sensations that leave a lasting impression. Each spoonful invites you to savor the velvety smoothness, the delicate sweetness, and the hint of tanginess that make Cheesecake Pudding an irresistible treat.

Section 1.4: Ingredients and Equipment

Creating a delectable Cheesecake Pudding requires the right combination of high-quality ingredients and appropriate tools. In this section, we delve into the essential components that form the foundation of Cheesecake Pudding. From cream cheese and eggs to sugar, vanilla extract, and more, we explore the key ingredients that contribute to the creamy and flavorful nature of this dessert. Each ingredient plays a vital role in achieving the desired texture and taste, ensuring that every spoonful is a delightful indulgence.

The choice of cream cheese is crucial, as it serves as the main component that imparts the distinct cheesecake flavor. Look for a creamy and smooth variety that will blend effortlessly with other ingredients. Eggs add richness and structure, providing the necessary stability for the pudding layer. Sugar adds sweetness, while vanilla extract enhances the overall flavor profile. Depending on the desired variations, additional ingredients such as fruits, chocolates, nuts, or spices can be incorporated to elevate the taste and create unique combinations.

Additionally, we discuss the necessary equipment and tools, such as mixing bowls, a whisk, and a springform pan, to ensure successful and visually appealing Cheesecake Pudding creations. Proper equipment allows for the smooth incorporation of ingredients and the precise execution of techniques, resulting in perfectly creamy and evenly baked Cheesecake Puddings. A springform pan facilitates easy removal of the desserts, while a whisk ensures thorough mixing and aeration of the batter. Each tool plays a crucial role in the preparation process, contributing to the ultimate success of your Cheesecake Pudding creations.

Through this introduction to Cheesecake Pudding, we have set the stage for an exciting culinary adventure. In the following chapters, we will explore a wide range of Cheesecake Pudding recipes, from classic flavors to innovative twists. Get ready to indulge in the velvety smoothness, heavenly flavors, and irresistible charm that Cheesecake Pudding brings to the dessert table. Each recipe will allow you to explore the endless possibilities and experience the joy of creating this delightful fusion of cheesecake and pudding. So, grab your ingredients, prepare your tools, and let's embark on a mouthwatering journey through the world of Cheesecake Pudding.

Chapter 2: The Basics of Cheesecake Pudding

Section 2.1: Understanding the Elements of Cheesecake Pudding

Cheesecake Pudding relies on a few key ingredients that work harmoniously to create its delightful texture and flavor. Cream cheese serves as the star ingredient, providing a rich, creamy base for the dessert. The cream cheese adds a tangy and slightly tart flavor that perfectly complements the sweetness of the other components. It also contributes to the smooth and velvety texture that is characteristic of Cheesecake Pudding.

Sweeteners, such as granulated sugar or confectioners' sugar, play a vital role in balancing the flavors of Cheesecake Pudding. Granulated sugar adds sweetness and helps create a creamy texture, while confectioners' sugar lends a smoother consistency and a more delicate sweetness. The choice of sweetener depends on personal preference and the desired level of sweetness.

Eggs are essential for achieving the perfect texture in Cheesecake Pudding. They provide structure and stability to the dessert, ensuring a smooth and silky consistency. When beaten or whisked, eggs also incorporate air into the mixture, resulting in a lighter and fluffier pudding. The eggs work together with the cream cheese to create a velvety texture that melts in your mouth with each spoonful.

Flavorings, such as vanilla extract, are added to enhance the overall taste of Cheesecake Pudding. Vanilla extract, with its warm and aromatic notes, is the most common flavoring used in Cheesecake Pudding recipes. It adds a touch of sweetness and a delightful fragrance that complements the creamy base. Other extracts, such as almond, lemon, or coconut, can be used to introduce unique flavor profiles and create exciting variations of Cheesecake Pudding.

Section 2.2: Selecting the Perfect Cream Cheese

Choosing the right cream cheese is essential for achieving the desired texture and taste in your Cheesecake Pudding. Regular cream cheese is the most commonly used option, offering a rich and creamy consistency that provides a solid foundation for the dessert. It has a slightly tangy flavor that enhances the overall taste of the pudding. Whipped cream cheese, on the other hand, is lighter and fluffier in texture, resulting in a softer and more delicate Cheesecake Pudding. Neufchâtel cheese, with its lower fat content compared to regular cream cheese, offers a slightly tangier flavor and can be used as a lighter alternative without compromising on taste.

When selecting cream cheese, look for a product that is smooth and creamy, without any lumps or graininess. The texture should be spreadable and easily incorporated into the other ingredients. Opt for a high-quality brand that ensures the cream cheese is fresh and free from any artificial additives.

Section 2.3: The Role of Sweeteners in Cheesecake Pudding

Sweeteners play a vital role in Cheesecake Pudding by adding the perfect level of sweetness and balancing the flavors. Granulated sugar is a common choice and provides a straightforward sweetness that enhances the creamy and tangy characteristics of the pudding. It also aids in creating a smooth and velvety texture. Confectioners' sugar, also known as powdered sugar, is finely ground and dissolves quickly, resulting in a smoother consistency and a delicate sweetness that blends seamlessly with the other ingredients.

For those seeking natural alternatives or specific dietary considerations, honey can be used as a sweetener in Cheesecake Pudding. Honey adds a distinct flavor and offers a natural sweetness that pairs well with the creamy base. Alternative sweeteners like maple syrup or agave nectar can also be used, providing different flavor profiles and catering to specific dietary needs. When using alternative sweeteners, adjustments may be necessary to maintain the desired consistency and sweetness of the pudding.

The amount of sweetener used in Cheesecake Pudding can be adjusted according to personal taste preferences. Start with the recommended amount in the recipe and taste the mixture before baking or chilling. Add more sweetener if a sweeter flavor is desired or reduce the amount if a lighter, less sweet pudding is preferred.

Section 2.4: Achieving the Perfect Texture with Eggs

Eggs are an essential component in Cheesecake Pudding, contributing to its smooth and velvety texture. They provide structure and stability to the pudding, helping it set and maintain its shape. The proteins in the eggs coagulate during baking or chilling, creating a firm yet creamy consistency.

The number of eggs used in Cheesecake Pudding recipes may vary depending on the desired texture and richness. Some recipes call for whole eggs, while others use a combination of whole eggs and egg yolks. The egg yolks add extra richness and contribute to the creamy texture, while the egg whites provide structure and stability.

When incorporating eggs into the cream cheese mixture, it's essential to do so gradually and with care. Beat or whisk the eggs lightly before adding them to the mixture to ensure even distribution. Overmixing the eggs can result in a denser and less smooth texture, while undermixing can lead to uneven incorporation and potential lumps.

Section 2.5: Flavor Enhancements with Extracts and Flavorings

While Cheesecake Pudding can be enjoyed with its classic vanilla flavor, it also offers endless possibilities for creative variations. Vanilla extract is the most commonly used flavoring in Cheesecake Pudding recipes. Its warm and aromatic notes complement the creamy base and add a delightful sweetness. The intensity of the vanilla flavor can be adjusted according to personal preference, with a small amount providing a subtle essence and a larger amount imparting a bolder flavor.

In addition to vanilla extract, other extracts can be used to infuse Cheesecake Pudding with unique flavors. Almond extract lends a nutty and sweet taste, enhancing the overall richness of the dessert. Citrus extracts, such as lemon or orange, bring a refreshing and tangy twist that balances the creaminess of the pudding. For those who crave a decadent chocolate experience, cocoa powder or melted chocolate can be added to create a chocolate Cheesecake Pudding. Experiment with different extracts and flavorings to discover your favorite combinations and create Cheesecake Puddings that cater to your personal taste preferences.

When adding flavorings, it's important to incorporate them at the right stage of the mixing process. Typically, extracts are added after the cream cheese and sweeteners have been combined and beaten together. This ensures that the flavorings are evenly dispersed throughout the mixture, resulting in a consistent and well-balanced flavor profile. Add the flavorings gradually, tasting the mixture as you go, to achieve the desired intensity of flavor.

Section 2.6: Mastering the Mixing Techniques

Mastering the mixing techniques is crucial to achieving a smooth and well-blended Cheesecake Pudding. Each step plays a significant role in creating a creamy and velvety texture.

When working with cream cheese, it's important to ensure that it is at room temperature before incorporating it into the other ingredients. This allows for easier blending and a smoother texture. Begin by beating or creaming the cream cheese until it is soft and smooth, without any lumps. This step can be done using a hand mixer or stand mixer, or even by hand using a sturdy whisk.

Once the cream cheese is smooth, gradually add the sweeteners and continue to mix until they are fully incorporated. Be sure to scrape down the sides of the bowl to ensure all the ingredients are well combined. Take care not to overmix at this stage, as it can lead to a denser texture.

When adding the eggs, lightly beat or whisk them before incorporating them into the cream cheese mixture. Gradually add the eggs, allowing them to blend in completely before adding more. This ensures that the eggs are evenly distributed throughout the pudding, contributing to a smooth and uniform texture. Again, avoid overmixing to prevent incorporating excess air into the mixture, which can result in a cracked or puffy surface during baking.

Finally, add the flavorings, such as vanilla extract or other extracts, to the mixture and gently mix until they are fully incorporated. This step should be done with a light hand to avoid overmixing.

Section 2.7: Baking and Cooling Techniques

Baking and cooling techniques are crucial to achieving the perfect texture and consistency in Cheesecake Pudding.

When it comes to baking, preheat the oven to the recommended temperature in the recipe. For even baking and to prevent cracking, consider using a water bath or bain-marie. This involves placing the filled baking dish or springform pan in a larger pan filled with hot water, creating a gentle and even heat distribution around the pudding. The water bath helps prevent overcooking and provides a moist environment, resulting in a creamy and smooth texture. It also reduces the likelihood of the top surface cracking during baking.

The baking time will vary depending on the recipe and the size of the pudding. Follow the instructions provided, and check for doneness by gently shaking the pan. The edges should be set while the center may still have a slight jiggle. Avoid overbaking, as it can lead to a dry and firm texture.

Once the Cheesecake Pudding is baked, it needs to be properly cooled to set and develop its signature silky texture. Allow the pudding to cool at room temperature for some time before transferring it to the refrigerator. This gradual cooling helps prevent rapid temperature changes, which can cause the surface to crack. Once cooled to room temperature, place the pudding in the refrigerator to chill and firm up. The cooling process can take several hours or overnight, depending on the recipe. Ensure the pudding is thoroughly chilled before serving to achieve the desired texture.

By mastering the basics of Cheesecake Pudding, you establish a solid foundation for creating a wide range of exquisite variations and indulgent desserts. The next chapters will explore classic flavors, innovative twists, and creative combinations, allowing you to unleash your culinary creativity and delight in the creamy decadence of Cheesecake Pudding. Get ready to elevate your dessert repertoire as we continue our exploration into the world of Cheesecake Pudding and discover endless possibilities for creamy delights.

Chapter 3: Classic Cheesecake Pudding Recipes

Section 3.1: Classic Vanilla Cheesecake Pudding

Indulge in the timeless elegance of Classic Vanilla Cheesecake Pudding. This recipe captures the essence of traditional cheesecake with a silky smooth pudding twist. Creamy, rich, and infused with the delicate fragrance of vanilla, this dessert is a true delight for the taste buds.

Ingredients:

- 8 ounces (225g) cream cheese, softened
- 1/2 cup (100g) granulated sugar
- 2 cups (480ml) whole milk
- 3 tablespoons cornstarch
- 1/4 teaspoon salt
- 2 teaspoons vanilla extract
- Whipped cream, for garnish (optional)
- Fresh berries, for garnish (optional)

Instructions:

1. In a mixing bowl, beat the cream cheese and sugar together until smooth and creamy.
2. In a separate saucepan, combine the milk, cornstarch, and salt. Whisk until the cornstarch is fully dissolved.
3. Place the saucepan over medium heat and cook, stirring constantly, until the mixture thickens and comes to a gentle boil.
4. Remove the saucepan from the heat. Gradually pour the hot

milk mixture into the cream cheese mixture, whisking continuously to ensure a smooth incorporation.

5. Return the mixture to the saucepan and place it back on the heat. Cook over medium heat, stirring constantly, until the pudding reaches a thick and creamy consistency.

6. Remove the saucepan from the heat and stir in the vanilla extract.

7. Pour the pudding into individual serving dishes or a large serving bowl. Allow it to cool to room temperature, then cover with plastic wrap and refrigerate for at least 2 hours, or until thoroughly chilled and set.

8. Before serving, garnish with whipped cream and fresh berries, if desired. Enjoy the classic flavors of vanilla cheesecake in a lusciously creamy pudding form.

Section 3.2: Decadent Chocolate Cheesecake Pudding

For chocolate lovers seeking a heavenly combination, Decadent Chocolate Cheesecake Pudding is a dream come true. The velvety smoothness of the cheesecake base is enriched with the irresistible allure of deep, dark chocolate. Each spoonful promises a harmonious fusion of creamy indulgence and intense chocolate flavor.

Ingredients:

- 8 ounces (225g) cream cheese, softened
- 1/2 cup (100g) granulated sugar
- 2 cups (480ml) whole milk
- 3 tablespoons cornstarch
- 1/4 teaspoon salt
- 2 teaspoons vanilla extract
- 4 ounces (115g) semi-sweet chocolate, finely chopped
- Whipped cream, for garnish (optional)
- Chocolate shavings, for garnish (optional)

Instructions:

1. In a mixing bowl, beat the cream cheese and sugar together until smooth and creamy.
2. In a separate saucepan, combine the milk, cornstarch, salt, and vanilla extract. Whisk until the cornstarch is fully dissolved.
3. Place the saucepan over medium heat and cook, stirring constantly, until the mixture thickens and comes to a gentle boil.
4. Remove the saucepan from the heat. Add the chopped chocolate to the hot milk mixture and stir until completely melted and incorporated.

5. Gradually pour the chocolate mixture into the cream cheese mixture, whisking continuously to ensure a smooth incorporation.

6. Return the mixture to the saucepan and place it back on the heat. Cook over medium heat, stirring constantly, until the pudding reaches a thick and creamy consistency.

7. Remove the saucepan from the heat and let the pudding cool for a few minutes.

8. Pour the pudding into individual serving dishes or a large serving bowl. Allow it to cool to room temperature, then cover with plastic wrap and refrigerate for at least 2 hours, or until thoroughly chilled and set.

9. Before serving, garnish with whipped cream and chocolate shavings, if desired. Savor the decadent combination of chocolate and cheesecake in a luxurious pudding form.

Enjoy these classic Cheesecake Pudding recipes as a delightful finale to any meal or as a special treat for Cheesecake and Pudding enthusiasts. The creamy textures and delicious flavors will leave you craving for more.

Chapter 4: Fruity Bliss: Fruit-Infused Cheesecake Pudding
Section 4.1: Strawberry Cheesecake Pudding

Embrace the vibrant taste of summer with Strawberry Cheesecake Pudding. This fruity delight combines the creamy goodness of cheesecake with the sweet and tangy essence of fresh strawberries. Each spoonful is a burst of fruity bliss that will leave you craving for more.

Ingredients:

- 8 ounces (225g) cream cheese, softened
- 1/2 cup (100g) granulated sugar
- 2 cups (480ml) whole milk
- 3 tablespoons cornstarch
- 1/4 teaspoon salt
- 1 cup fresh strawberries, hulled and diced
- 1 teaspoon lemon zest (optional)
- Whipped cream, for garnish (optional)
- Fresh strawberry slices, for garnish (optional)

Instructions:

1. In a mixing bowl, beat the cream cheese and sugar together until smooth and creamy.
2. In a separate saucepan, combine the milk, cornstarch, and salt. Whisk until the cornstarch is fully dissolved.
3. Place the saucepan over medium heat and cook, stirring constantly, until the mixture thickens and comes to a gentle boil.
4. Remove the saucepan from the heat. Gradually pour the hot

milk mixture into the cream cheese mixture, whisking continuously to ensure a smooth incorporation.

5. Return the mixture to the saucepan and place it back on the heat. Cook over medium heat, stirring constantly, until the pudding reaches a thick and creamy consistency.

6. Remove the saucepan from the heat and let the pudding cool for a few minutes.

7. In a blender or food processor, puree the diced strawberries until smooth. If desired, add lemon zest for an extra burst of flavor and mix well.

8. Fold the strawberry puree into the cooled pudding mixture, gently swirling it in to create a marbled effect.

9. Pour the strawberry-infused pudding into individual serving dishes or a large serving bowl. Allow it to cool to room temperature, then cover with plastic wrap and refrigerate for at least 2 hours, or until thoroughly chilled and set.

10. Before serving, garnish with whipped cream and fresh strawberry slices, if desired. Experience the delightful combination of creamy cheesecake and luscious strawberries in every spoonful.

Section 4.2: Tropical Mango Cheesecake Pudding

Transport your taste buds to a tropical paradise with Mango Cheesecake Pudding. This exotic twist on classic cheesecake pudding features the heavenly sweetness and vibrant flavor of ripe mangoes. With each spoonful, you'll be immersed in a tropical symphony of creamy indulgence.

Ingredients:

- 8 ounces (225g) cream cheese, softened
- 1/2 cup (100g) granulated sugar
- 2 cups (480ml) whole milk
- 3 tablespoons cornstarch
- 1/4 teaspoon salt
- 1 cup ripe mango, peeled and diced
- 1 tablespoon lime juice (optional)
- Whipped cream, for garnish (optional)
- Fresh mango slices, for garnish (optional)

Instructions:

1. In a mixing bowl, beat the cream cheese and sugar together until smooth and creamy.
2. In a separate saucepan, combine the milk, cornstarch, and salt. Whisk until the cornstarch is fully dissolved.
3. Place the saucepan over medium heat and cook, stirring constantly, until the mixture thickens and comes to a gentle boil.
4. Remove the saucepan from the heat. Gradually pour the hot milk mixture into the cream cheese mixture, whisking continuously to ensure a smooth incorporation.

5. Return the mixture to the saucepan and place it back on the heat. Cook over medium heat, stirring constantly, until the pudding reaches a thick and creamy consistency.

6. Remove the saucepan from the heat and let the pudding cool for a few minutes.

7. In a blender or food processor, puree the diced mango until smooth. If desired, add lime juice for a tangy twist and mix well.

8. Fold the mango puree into the cooled pudding mixture, gently swirling it in to create a marbled effect.

9. Pour the mango-infused pudding into individual serving dishes or a large serving bowl. Allow it to cool to room temperature, then cover with plastic wrap and refrigerate for at least 2 hours, or until thoroughly chilled and set.

10. Before serving, garnish with whipped cream and fresh mango slices, if desired. Immerse yourself in the tropical flavors of creamy cheesecake and juicy mangoes with every spoonful.

Enjoy the delightful combination of creamy cheesecake pudding and the freshness of seasonal fruits. These fruit-infused variations bring a burst of flavor and a touch of brightness to your dessert table.

Chapter 5: Chocolate Lover's Paradise: Decadent Chocolate Cheesecake Pudding

Section 5.1: Dark Chocolate Cheesecake Pudding

Experience pure decadence with Dark Chocolate Cheesecake Pudding. This recipe takes chocolate lovers to a whole new level of bliss. Rich, velvety, and intensely chocolaty, each spoonful is a symphony of flavors that will satisfy your deepest chocolate cravings.

Ingredients:

- 8 ounces (225g) cream cheese, softened
- 1/2 cup (100g) granulated sugar
- 2 cups (480ml) whole milk
- 3 tablespoons cornstarch
- 1/4 teaspoon salt
- 4 ounces (115g) dark chocolate, finely chopped
- 1 teaspoon vanilla extract
- Whipped cream, for garnish (optional)
- Chocolate shavings, for garnish (optional)

Instructions:

1. In a mixing bowl, beat the cream cheese and sugar together until smooth and creamy.
2. In a separate saucepan, combine the milk, cornstarch, and salt. Whisk until the cornstarch is fully dissolved.
3. Place the saucepan over medium heat and cook, stirring constantly, until the mixture thickens and comes to a gentle boil.

4. Remove the saucepan from the heat. Add the chopped dark chocolate to the hot milk mixture and stir until completely melted and incorporated.

5. Gradually pour the chocolate mixture into the cream cheese mixture, whisking continuously to ensure a smooth incorporation.

6. Return the mixture to the saucepan and place it back on the heat. Cook over medium heat, stirring constantly, until the pudding reaches a thick and creamy consistency.

7. Remove the saucepan from the heat and stir in the vanilla extract.

8. Pour the chocolate-infused pudding into individual serving dishes or a large serving bowl. Allow it to cool to room temperature, then cover with plastic wrap and refrigerate for at least 2 hours, or until thoroughly chilled and set.

9. Before serving, garnish with whipped cream and chocolate shavings, if desired. Dive into the ultimate chocolate indulgence with each spoonful of this dark chocolate cheesecake pudding.

Section 5.2: White Chocolate Raspberry Cheesecake Pudding

Delight in the irresistible combination of white chocolate and raspberries with White Chocolate Raspberry Cheesecake Pudding. The sweet creaminess of white chocolate blends harmoniously with the tartness of fresh raspberries, creating a dessert that is both luxurious and refreshing.

Ingredients:

- 8 ounces (225g) cream cheese, softened
- 1/2 cup (100g) granulated sugar
- 2 cups (480ml) whole milk
- 3 tablespoons cornstarch
- 1/4 teaspoon salt
- 4 ounces (115g) white chocolate, finely chopped
- 1 teaspoon vanilla extract
- 1 cup fresh raspberries, divided
- Whipped cream, for garnish (optional)
- Fresh raspberries, for garnish (optional)

Instructions:

1. In a mixing bowl, beat the cream cheese and sugar together until smooth and creamy.
2. In a separate saucepan, combine the milk, cornstarch, and salt. Whisk until the cornstarch is fully dissolved.
3. Place the saucepan over medium heat and cook, stirring constantly, until the mixture thickens and comes to a gentle boil.
4. Remove the saucepan from the heat. Add the chopped white chocolate to the hot milk mixture and stir until completely

melted and incorporated.

5. Gradually pour the chocolate mixture into the cream cheese mixture, whisking continuously to ensure a smooth incorporation.

6. Return the mixture to the saucepan and place it back on the heat. Cook over medium heat, stirring constantly, until the pudding reaches a thick and creamy consistency.

7. Remove the saucepan from the heat and stir in the vanilla extract.

8. In a small bowl, mash half of the fresh raspberries with a fork to release their juices.

9. Fold the mashed raspberries into the pudding mixture, creating a beautiful swirl.

10. Pour the white chocolate and raspberry-infused pudding into individual serving dishes or a large serving bowl. Allow it to cool to room temperature, then cover with plastic wrap and refrigerate for at least 2 hours, or until thoroughly chilled and set.

11. Before serving, garnish with whipped cream and fresh raspberries, if desired. Delight in the luxurious combination of white chocolate and tart raspberries in this decadent cheesecake pudding.

Indulge in the ultimate chocolate experience with these delectable chocolate cheesecake pudding recipes. Whether you prefer the rich intensity of dark chocolate or the creamy sweetness of white chocolate, these recipes will satisfy your cravings and transport you to a chocolate lover's paradise.

Chapter 6: Nutty Twists: Nut-Infused Cheesecake Pudding Delights

Section 6.1: Hazelnut Praline Cheesecake Pudding

Indulge in the rich and nutty flavors of Hazelnut Praline Cheesecake Pudding. This delightful dessert combines the smooth creaminess of cheesecake with the irresistible crunch and toasty aroma of hazelnuts. Each spoonful is a symphony of flavors that will transport you to a world of nut-infused bliss.

Ingredients:

- 8 ounces (225g) cream cheese, softened
- 1/2 cup (100g) granulated sugar
- 2 cups (480ml) whole milk
- 3 tablespoons cornstarch
- 1/4 teaspoon salt
- 1/2 cup hazelnuts, toasted and finely chopped
- 1 teaspoon vanilla extract
- Whipped cream, for garnish (optional)
- Hazelnut praline, for garnish (optional)

Instructions:

1. In a mixing bowl, beat the cream cheese and sugar together until smooth and creamy.
2. In a separate saucepan, combine the milk, cornstarch, and salt. Whisk until the cornstarch is fully dissolved.
3. Place the saucepan over medium heat and cook, stirring constantly, until the mixture thickens and comes to a gentle boil.

4. Remove the saucepan from the heat. Gradually pour the hot milk mixture into the cream cheese mixture, whisking continuously to ensure a smooth incorporation.

5. Return the mixture to the saucepan and place it back on the heat. Cook over medium heat, stirring constantly, until the pudding reaches a thick and creamy consistency.

6. Remove the saucepan from the heat and let the pudding cool for a few minutes.

7. Stir in the finely chopped toasted hazelnuts and vanilla extract, ensuring they are evenly distributed throughout the pudding.

8. Pour the hazelnut-infused pudding into individual serving dishes or a large serving bowl. Allow it to cool to room temperature, then cover with plastic wrap and refrigerate for at least 2 hours, or until thoroughly chilled and set.

9. Before serving, garnish with whipped cream and a sprinkle of hazelnut praline, if desired. Savor the delightful combination of creamy cheesecake and the nutty essence of hazelnuts in every spoonful.

Section 6.2: Almond Joy Cheesecake Pudding

Experience the irresistible flavors of Almond Joy in cheesecake pudding form with Almond Joy Cheesecake Pudding. This nut-infused delight combines the creamy goodness of cheesecake with the heavenly trio of almonds, coconut, and chocolate. Indulge in the nutty twists of this dessert and let your taste buds be swept away.

Ingredients:

- 8 ounces (225g) cream cheese, softened
- 1/2 cup (100g) granulated sugar
- 2 cups (480ml) whole milk
- 3 tablespoons cornstarch
- 1/4 teaspoon salt
- 1/4 cup shredded coconut
- 1/4 cup chopped almonds
- 2 tablespoons cocoa powder
- 1 teaspoon almond extract
- Whipped cream, for garnish (optional)
- Toasted coconut flakes, for garnish (optional)
- Chocolate shavings, for garnish (optional)

Instructions:

1. In a mixing bowl, beat the cream cheese and sugar together until smooth and creamy.
2. In a separate saucepan, combine the milk, cornstarch, and salt. Whisk until the cornstarch is fully dissolved.
3. Place the saucepan over medium heat and cook, stirring constantly, until the mixture thickens and comes to a gentle boil.

4. Remove the saucepan from the heat. Gradually pour the hot milk mixture into the cream cheese mixture, whisking continuously to ensure a smooth incorporation.

5. Return the mixture to the saucepan and place it back on the heat. Cook over medium heat, stirring constantly, until the pudding reaches a thick and creamy consistency.

6. Remove the saucepan from the heat and let the pudding cool for a few minutes.

7. Stir in the shredded coconut, chopped almonds, cocoa powder, and almond extract until well combined.

8. Pour the Almond Joy-infused pudding into individual serving dishes or a large serving bowl. Allow it to cool to room temperature, then cover with plastic wrap and refrigerate for at least 2 hours, or until thoroughly chilled and set.

9. Before serving, garnish with whipped cream, toasted coconut flakes, and chocolate shavings, if desired. Delight in the nutty twist of Almond Joy combined with the creamy indulgence of cheesecake in each spoonful.

Discover the nutty goodness of these nut-infused cheesecake pudding delights. Whether you prefer the rich and toasty flavor of hazelnuts or the blissful combination of almonds, coconut, and chocolate, these recipes will satisfy your cravings and take your taste buds on a nutty journey.

Chapter 7: Seasonal Sensations: Cheesecake Pudding for Every Season

Section 7.1: Springtime Lemon Cheesecake Pudding

Welcome the freshness of spring with Springtime Lemon Cheesecake Pudding. This light and tangy dessert captures the essence of the season with its bright citrus flavors. Each spoonful will transport you to a sunny garden and leave you feeling refreshed and satisfied.

Ingredients:

- 8 ounces (225g) cream cheese, softened
- 1/2 cup (100g) granulated sugar
- 2 cups (480ml) whole milk
- 3 tablespoons cornstarch
- 1/4 teaspoon salt
- Zest of 2 lemons
- 1/4 cup freshly squeezed lemon juice
- Whipped cream, for garnish (optional)
- Lemon zest, for garnish (optional)

Instructions:

1. In a mixing bowl, beat the cream cheese and sugar together until smooth and creamy.
2. In a separate saucepan, combine the milk, cornstarch, and salt. Whisk until the cornstarch is fully dissolved.
3. Place the saucepan over medium heat and cook, stirring constantly, until the mixture thickens and comes to a gentle boil.
4. Remove the saucepan from the heat. Gradually pour the hot

milk mixture into the cream cheese mixture, whisking continuously to ensure a smooth incorporation.

5. Return the mixture to the saucepan and place it back on the heat. Cook over medium heat, stirring constantly, until the pudding reaches a thick and creamy consistency.

6. Remove the saucepan from the heat and let the pudding cool for a few minutes.

7. Stir in the lemon zest and freshly squeezed lemon juice until well combined.

8. Pour the lemon-infused pudding into individual serving dishes or a large serving bowl. Allow it to cool to room temperature, then cover with plastic wrap and refrigerate for at least 2 hours, or until thoroughly chilled and set.

9. Before serving, garnish with whipped cream and a sprinkle of lemon zest, if desired. Embrace the bright and refreshing flavors of spring with each spoonful of this lemon cheesecake pudding.

Section 7.2: Summertime Berry Cheesecake Pudding

Celebrate the abundance of summer berries with Summertime Berry Cheesecake Pudding. This fruity and vibrant dessert showcases the lusciousness of seasonal berries, bringing a burst of sweetness to every spoonful. Enjoy the taste of summer in this delightful cheesecake pudding.

Ingredients:

- 8 ounces (225g) cream cheese, softened
- 1/2 cup (100g) granulated sugar
- 2 cups (480ml) whole milk
- 3 tablespoons cornstarch
- 1/4 teaspoon salt
- 1 cup mixed fresh berries (such as strawberries, blueberries, raspberries)
- 1 tablespoon lemon juice
- Whipped cream, for garnish (optional)
- Fresh berries, for garnish (optional)

Instructions:

1. In a mixing bowl, beat the cream cheese and sugar together until smooth and creamy.
2. In a separate saucepan, combine the milk, cornstarch, and salt. Whisk until the cornstarch is fully dissolved.
3. Place the saucepan over medium heat and cook, stirring constantly, until the mixture thickens and comes to a gentle boil.
4. Remove the saucepan from the heat. Gradually pour the hot milk mixture into the cream cheese mixture, whisking

continuously to ensure a smooth incorporation.

5. Return the mixture to the saucepan and place it back on the heat. Cook over medium heat, stirring constantly, until the pudding reaches a thick and creamy consistency.

6. Remove the saucepan from the heat and let the pudding cool for a few minutes.

7. In a blender or food processor, puree half of the mixed fresh berries until smooth. Stir in the lemon juice.

8. Fold the berry puree into the cooled pudding mixture, gently swirling it in to create a marbled effect.

9. Pour the berry-infused pudding into individual serving dishes or a large serving bowl. Allow it to cool to room temperature, then cover with plastic wrap and refrigerate for at least 2 hours, or until thoroughly chilled and set.

10. Before serving, garnish with whipped cream and fresh berries, if desired. Enjoy the delightful taste of summer with each spoonful of this berry cheesecake pudding.

Section 7.3: Autumn Spice Cheesecake Pudding

Embrace the warm and comforting flavors of autumn with Autumn Spice Cheesecake Pudding. This dessert captures the essence of the season with its aromatic spices and cozy notes. Let each spoonful transport you to a crisp fall day filled with delightful flavors.

Ingredients:

- 8 ounces (225g) cream cheese, softened
- 1/2 cup (100g) granulated sugar
- 2 cups (480ml) whole milk
- 3 tablespoons cornstarch
- 1/4 teaspoon salt
- 1 teaspoon ground cinnamon
- 1/2 teaspoon ground nutmeg
- 1/4 teaspoon ground cloves
- 1/4 teaspoon ground ginger
- Whipped cream, for garnish (optional)
- Ground cinnamon, for garnish (optional)

Instructions:

1. In a mixing bowl, beat the cream cheese and sugar together until smooth and creamy.
2. In a separate saucepan, combine the milk, cornstarch, salt, and spices (cinnamon, nutmeg, cloves, ginger). Whisk until the cornstarch is fully dissolved and the spices are well combined.
3. Place the saucepan over medium heat and cook, stirring constantly, until the mixture thickens and comes to a gentle boil.
4. Remove the saucepan from the heat. Gradually pour the hot

milk mixture into the cream cheese mixture, whisking continuously to ensure a smooth incorporation.

5. Return the mixture to the saucepan and place it back on the heat. Cook over medium heat, stirring constantly, until the pudding reaches a thick and creamy consistency.

6. Remove the saucepan from the heat and let the pudding cool for a few minutes.

7. Pour the spiced-infused pudding into individual serving dishes or a large serving bowl. Allow it to cool to room temperature, then cover with plastic wrap and refrigerate for at least 2 hours, or until thoroughly chilled and set.

8. Before serving, garnish with whipped cream and a sprinkle of ground cinnamon, if desired. Delight in the warm and cozy flavors of autumn with each spoonful of this spiced cheesecake pudding.

Section 7.4: Winter Wonderland Peppermint Cheesecake Pudding

Embrace the cool and refreshing flavors of winter with Winter Wonderland Peppermint Cheesecake Pudding. This dessert captures the magic of the season with its minty freshness and indulgent creaminess. Each spoonful will transport you to a snowy wonderland of delightful flavors.

Ingredients:

- 8 ounces (225g) cream cheese, softened
- 1/2 cup (100g) granulated sugar
- 2 cups (480ml) whole milk
- 3 tablespoons cornstarch
- 1/4 teaspoon salt
- 1 teaspoon peppermint extract
- Crushed candy canes, for garnish (optional)
- Whipped cream, for garnish (optional)

Instructions:

1. In a mixing bowl, beat the cream cheese and sugar together until smooth and creamy.
2. In a separate saucepan, combine the milk, cornstarch, and salt. Whisk until the cornstarch is fully dissolved.
3. Place the saucepan over medium heat and cook, stirring constantly, until the mixture thickens and comes to a gentle boil.
4. Remove the saucepan from the heat. Gradually pour the hot milk mixture into the cream cheese mixture, whisking continuously to ensure a smooth incorporation.
5. Return the mixture to the saucepan and place it back on the

heat. Cook over medium heat, stirring constantly, until the pudding reaches a thick and creamy consistency.

6. Remove the saucepan from the heat and let the pudding cool for a few minutes.

7. Stir in the peppermint extract until well combined.

8. Pour the peppermint-infused pudding into individual serving dishes or a large serving bowl. Allow it to cool to room temperature, then cover with plastic wrap and refrigerate for at least 2 hours, or until thoroughly chilled and set.

9. Before serving, garnish with whipped cream and a sprinkle of crushed candy canes, if desired. Let the refreshing flavors of peppermint transport you to a winter wonderland with each spoonful of this peppermint cheesecake pudding.

Celebrate the flavors of each season with these delightful seasonal cheesecake pudding recipes. Whether it's the bright and tangy lemon of spring, the vibrant berries of summer, the warm spices of autumn, or the refreshing peppermint of winter, these recipes will evoke the essence of each season and leave you with a smile on your face.

Chapter 8: Exotic Variations: International Cheesecake Pudding Recipes

Section 8.1: Matcha Green Tea Cheesecake Pudding (Japan)

Experience the elegance and earthy flavors of Japan with Matcha Green Tea Cheesecake Pudding. This unique dessert combines the smoothness of cheesecake with the distinct taste of matcha green tea, resulting in a harmonious balance of creamy indulgence and refreshing bitterness.

Ingredients:

- 8 ounces (225g) cream cheese, softened
- 1/2 cup (100g) granulated sugar
- 2 cups (480ml) whole milk
- 3 tablespoons cornstarch
- 1/4 teaspoon salt
- 2 tablespoons matcha green tea powder
- Whipped cream, for garnish (optional)
- Matcha powder, for garnish (optional)

Instructions:

1. In a mixing bowl, beat the cream cheese and sugar together until smooth and creamy.
2. In a separate saucepan, combine the milk, cornstarch, and salt. Whisk until the cornstarch is fully dissolved.
3. Place the saucepan over medium heat and cook, stirring constantly, until the mixture thickens and comes to a gentle boil.

4. Remove the saucepan from the heat. Gradually pour the hot milk mixture into the cream cheese mixture, whisking continuously to ensure a smooth incorporation.
5. Return the mixture to the saucepan and place it back on the heat. Cook over medium heat, stirring constantly, until the pudding reaches a thick and creamy consistency.
6. Remove the saucepan from the heat and let the pudding cool for a few minutes.
7. Sift the matcha green tea powder into the cooled pudding mixture and whisk until well combined.
8. Pour the matcha-infused pudding into individual serving dishes or a large serving bowl. Allow it to cool to room temperature, then cover with plastic wrap and refrigerate for at least 2 hours, or until thoroughly chilled and set.
9. Before serving, garnish with whipped cream and a sprinkle of matcha powder, if desired. Immerse yourself in the unique flavors of Japan with each spoonful of this matcha green tea cheesecake pudding.

Section 8.2: Tiramisu Cheesecake Pudding (Italy)

Indulge in the decadent flavors of Italy with Tiramisu Cheesecake Pudding. This fusion of two beloved desserts, cheesecake, and tiramisu, creates a luscious and creamy delight. With layers of ladyfingers soaked in coffee and a hint of cocoa, this dessert will transport you to the charming streets of Italy.

Ingredients:

- 8 ounces (225g) cream cheese, softened
- 1/2 cup (100g) granulated sugar
- 2 cups (480ml) whole milk
- 3 tablespoons cornstarch
- 1/4 teaspoon salt
- 1/2 cup strong brewed coffee, cooled
- 1/4 cup coffee liqueur (such as Kahlua) (optional)
- 12 ladyfingers, halved
- Cocoa powder, for dusting
- Whipped cream, for garnish (optional)

Instructions:

1. In a mixing bowl, beat the cream cheese and sugar together until smooth and creamy.
2. In a separate saucepan, combine the milk, cornstarch, and salt. Whisk until the cornstarch is fully dissolved.
3. Place the saucepan over medium heat and cook, stirring constantly, until the mixture thickens and comes to a gentle boil.
4. Remove the saucepan from the heat. Gradually pour the hot milk mixture into the cream cheese mixture, whisking

continuously to ensure a smooth incorporation.

5. Return the mixture to the saucepan and place it back on the heat. Cook over medium heat, stirring constantly, until the pudding reaches a thick and creamy consistency.

6. Remove the saucepan from the heat and let the pudding cool for a few minutes.

7. In a shallow dish, combine the cooled coffee and coffee liqueur, if using.

8. Dip each ladyfinger half into the coffee mixture, briefly soaking it, and arrange them in a layer at the bottom of individual serving dishes or a large serving bowl.

9. Pour the cheesecake pudding over the ladyfingers, creating a second layer.

10. Repeat the ladyfinger and pudding layers until all ingredients are used, ending with a layer of pudding.

11. Dust the top layer with cocoa powder.

12. Allow the tiramisu cheesecake pudding to cool to room temperature, then cover with plastic wrap and refrigerate for at least 4 hours, or overnight, to allow the flavors to meld together.

13. Before serving, garnish with whipped cream, if desired. Indulge in the luxurious flavors of Italy with each spoonful of this tiramisu cheesecake pudding.

Section 8.3: Coconut Pandan Cheesecake Pudding (Southeast Asia)

Embark on a flavor adventure to Southeast Asia with Coconut Pandan Cheesecake Pudding. This exotic dessert combines the creaminess of cheesecake with the aromatic flavors of coconut and pandan. Each spoonful will transport you to the tropical paradise of Southeast Asia.

Ingredients:

- 8 ounces (225g) cream cheese, softened
- 1/2 cup (100g) granulated sugar
- 2 cups (480ml) coconut milk
- 3 tablespoons cornstarch
- 1/4 teaspoon salt
- 1 teaspoon pandan extract
- Shredded coconut, for garnish (optional)

Instructions:

1. In a mixing bowl, beat the cream cheese and sugar together until smooth and creamy.
2. In a separate saucepan, combine the coconut milk, cornstarch, and salt. Whisk until the cornstarch is fully dissolved.
3. Place the saucepan over medium heat and cook, stirring constantly, until the mixture thickens and comes to a gentle boil.
4. Remove the saucepan from the heat. Gradually pour the hot coconut milk mixture into the cream cheese mixture, whisking continuously to ensure a smooth incorporation.
5. Return the mixture to the saucepan and place it back on the heat. Cook over medium heat, stirring constantly, until the pudding reaches a thick and creamy consistency.

6. Remove the saucepan from the heat and let the pudding cool for a few minutes.
7. Stir in the pandan extract until well combined.
8. Pour the coconut pandan-infused pudding into individual serving dishes or a large serving bowl. Allow it to cool to room temperature, then cover with plastic wrap and refrigerate for at least 2 hours, or until thoroughly chilled and set.
9. Before serving, garnish with shredded coconut, if desired. Embark on a culinary journey to Southeast Asia with each spoonful of this coconut pandan cheesecake pudding.

Explore the world through the flavors of these international cheesecake pudding recipes. Whether you're captivated by the earthiness of matcha from Japan, the richness of tiramisu from Italy, or the exotic combination of coconut and pandan from Southeast Asia, these recipes will take your taste buds on a global adventure.

Chapter 9: No-Bake Cheesecake Pudding Recipes

Section 9.1: Cookies and Cream Cheesecake Pudding

Indulge in the classic combination of cookies and cream with this No-Bake Cookies and Cream Cheesecake Pudding. With its creamy texture and delightful cookie crunch, this dessert is a crowd-pleaser that requires no baking, making it perfect for those hot summer days or any time you crave a delicious treat.

Ingredients:

- 8 ounces (225g) cream cheese, softened
- 1/2 cup (100g) granulated sugar
- 2 cups (480ml) heavy cream
- 1 teaspoon vanilla extract
- 1 cup crushed chocolate sandwich cookies
- Whipped cream, for garnish (optional)
- Crushed cookies, for garnish (optional)

Instructions:

1. In a mixing bowl, beat the cream cheese and sugar together until smooth and creamy.
2. In a separate mixing bowl, whip the heavy cream and vanilla extract until soft peaks form.
3. Gently fold the whipped cream into the cream cheese mixture until well combined.
4. Stir in the crushed chocolate sandwich cookies, reserving some for garnish if desired.
5. Spoon the cookies and cream cheesecake pudding into

individual serving dishes or a large serving bowl.

6. Refrigerate for at least 2 hours to allow the pudding to set and the flavors to meld together.

7. Before serving, garnish with a dollop of whipped cream and a sprinkle of crushed cookies, if desired. Enjoy the creamy, no-bake delight of this cookies and cream cheesecake pudding.

Section 9.2: Peanut Butter Chocolate Cheesecake Pudding

Satisfy your cravings for the classic combination of peanut butter and chocolate with this No-Bake Peanut Butter Chocolate Cheesecake Pudding. With its rich and indulgent flavors, this dessert is a heavenly treat that requires no baking, making it a quick and easy option for any occasion.

Ingredients:

- 8 ounces (225g) cream cheese, softened
- 1/2 cup (100g) powdered sugar
- 1 cup creamy peanut butter
- 2 cups (480ml) heavy cream
- 1 teaspoon vanilla extract
- 1/2 cup chocolate chips
- Whipped cream, for garnish (optional)
- Chocolate shavings, for garnish (optional)

Instructions:

1. In a mixing bowl, beat the cream cheese and powdered sugar together until smooth and creamy.
2. Add the peanut butter to the cream cheese mixture and beat until well combined.
3. In a separate mixing bowl, whip the heavy cream and vanilla extract until soft peaks form.
4. Gently fold the whipped cream into the peanut butter cream cheese mixture until well combined.
5. Stir in the chocolate chips, reserving some for garnish if desired.
6. Spoon the peanut butter chocolate cheesecake pudding into

individual serving dishes or a large serving bowl.

7. Refrigerate for at least 2 hours to allow the pudding to set and the flavors to meld together.

8. Before serving, garnish with a dollop of whipped cream and a sprinkle of chocolate shavings, if desired. Indulge in the decadent flavors of this no-bake peanut butter chocolate cheesecake pudding.

Section 9.3: Fresh Fruit Parfait Cheesecake Pudding

Create a refreshing and colorful dessert with this No-Bake Fresh Fruit Parfait Cheesecake Pudding. Layered with creamy cheesecake pudding and a variety of fresh fruits, this parfait is not only visually appealing but also bursting with fruity goodness. It's a delightful treat that requires no baking and is perfect for showcasing the vibrant flavors of seasonal fruits.

Ingredients:

- 8 ounces (225g) cream cheese, softened
- 1/2 cup (100g) granulated sugar
- 2 cups (480ml) heavy cream
- 1 teaspoon vanilla extract
- Assorted fresh fruits (such as berries, kiwi, pineapple, mango), sliced or diced
- Granola or crushed graham crackers, for layering
- Whipped cream, for garnish (optional)
- Fresh mint leaves, for garnish (optional)

Instructions:

1. In a mixing bowl, beat the cream cheese and sugar together until smooth and creamy.
2. In a separate mixing bowl, whip the heavy cream and vanilla extract until soft peaks form.
3. Gently fold the whipped cream into the cream cheese mixture until well combined.
4. Prepare an assortment of fresh fruits, washing, peeling, and slicing as needed.
5. In individual serving glasses or bowls, layer the cheesecake

pudding, fresh fruits, and granola or crushed graham crackers, repeating the layers until the glass or bowl is filled.
6. Repeat the layering process for each serving.
7. Refrigerate for at least 2 hours to allow the pudding to set and the flavors to meld together.
8. Before serving, garnish with a dollop of whipped cream and a fresh mint leaf, if desired. Enjoy the refreshing and fruity delight of this no-bake fresh fruit parfait cheesecake pudding.

Enjoy the convenience and deliciousness of these no-bake cheesecake pudding recipes. Whether you're a fan of cookies and cream, peanut butter and chocolate, or the freshness of fruit parfaits, these desserts are quick, easy, and perfect for satisfying your sweet tooth without turning on the oven.

Chapter 10: Miniature Indulgences: Cheesecake Pudding for Single Servings

Section 10.1: Mini Strawberry Cheesecake Pudding Cups

Indulge in the sweetness of strawberries with these Mini Strawberry Cheesecake Pudding Cups. These single-serving desserts are perfect for satisfying your cravings and enjoying a delightful portion of creamy cheesecake pudding topped with luscious strawberry goodness.

Ingredients:

- 4 ounces (113g) cream cheese, softened
- 1/4 cup (50g) granulated sugar
- 1/2 cup (120ml) whole milk
- 1 tablespoon cornstarch
- 1/4 teaspoon vanilla extract
- Fresh strawberries, sliced
- Graham cracker crumbs, for garnish (optional)

Instructions:

1. In a mixing bowl, beat the cream cheese and sugar together until smooth and creamy.
2. In a separate saucepan, combine the milk and cornstarch. Whisk until the cornstarch is fully dissolved.
3. Place the saucepan over medium heat and cook, stirring constantly, until the mixture thickens and comes to a gentle boil.
4. Remove the saucepan from the heat. Gradually pour the hot milk mixture into the cream cheese mixture, whisking continuously to ensure a smooth incorporation.

5. Stir in the vanilla extract until well combined.
6. Divide the cheesecake pudding mixture into individual serving cups or ramekins.
7. Allow the pudding to cool to room temperature, then cover with plastic wrap and refrigerate for at least 2 hours, or until thoroughly chilled and set.
8. Before serving, top each pudding cup with fresh strawberry slices and a sprinkle of graham cracker crumbs, if desired. Enjoy the delectable mini indulgence of these strawberry cheesecake pudding cups.

Section 10.2: Mini Salted Caramel Cheesecake Pudding Jars

Experience the perfect balance of sweetness and saltiness with these Mini Salted Caramel Cheesecake Pudding Jars. These single-serve desserts combine the creamy richness of cheesecake pudding with the irresistible allure of salted caramel, creating a delightful treat that's perfect for solo enjoyment.

Ingredients:

- 4 ounces (113g) cream cheese, softened
- 1/4 cup (50g) granulated sugar
- 1/2 cup (120ml) whole milk
- 1 tablespoon cornstarch
- 1/4 teaspoon vanilla extract
- Salted caramel sauce
- Sea salt flakes, for garnish (optional)

Instructions:

1. In a mixing bowl, beat the cream cheese and sugar together until smooth and creamy.
2. In a separate saucepan, combine the milk and cornstarch. Whisk until the cornstarch is fully dissolved.
3. Place the saucepan over medium heat and cook, stirring constantly, until the mixture thickens and comes to a gentle boil.
4. Remove the saucepan from the heat. Gradually pour the hot milk mixture into the cream cheese mixture, whisking continuously to ensure a smooth incorporation.
5. Stir in the vanilla extract until well combined.
6. Divide the cheesecake pudding mixture into individual

serving jars.

7. Allow the pudding to cool to room temperature, then cover with plastic wrap and refrigerate for at least 2 hours, or until thoroughly chilled and set.

8. Before serving, drizzle each jar with salted caramel sauce and sprinkle a pinch of sea salt flakes, if desired. Delight in the single-serve luxury of these salted caramel cheesecake pudding jars.

Section 10.3: Mini Chocolate Mint Cheesecake Pudding Jars

Indulge in the delightful combination of chocolate and mint with these Mini Chocolate Mint Cheesecake Pudding Jars. These individual treats layer creamy cheesecake pudding with rich chocolate and refreshing mint, creating a miniature indulgence that will satisfy your sweet tooth.

Ingredients:

- 4 ounces (113g) cream cheese, softened
- 1/4 cup (50g) granulated sugar
- 1/2 cup (120ml) whole milk
- 1 tablespoon cornstarch
- 1/4 teaspoon peppermint extract
- Chocolate sauce
- Fresh mint leaves, for garnish (optional)

Instructions:

1. In a mixing bowl, beat the cream cheese and sugar together until smooth and creamy.
2. In a separate saucepan, combine the milk and cornstarch. Whisk until the cornstarch is fully dissolved.
3. Place the saucepan over medium heat and cook, stirring constantly, until the mixture thickens and comes to a gentle boil.
4. Remove the saucepan from the heat. Gradually pour the hot milk mixture into the cream cheese mixture, whisking continuously to ensure a smooth incorporation.
5. Stir in the peppermint extract until well combined.
6. Divide the cheesecake pudding mixture into individual

serving jars.

7. Allow the pudding to cool to room temperature, then cover with plastic wrap and refrigerate for at least 2 hours, or until thoroughly chilled and set.

8. Before serving, drizzle each jar with chocolate sauce and garnish with a fresh mint leaf, if desired. Enjoy the miniature delight of these chocolate mint cheesecake pudding jars.

Savor the sweetness of these single-serving cheesecake pudding recipes. Whether you choose the fruity goodness of strawberry, the irresistible allure of salted caramel, or the classic combination of chocolate and mint, these mini indulgences are perfect for treating yourself to a delightful and personal dessert experience.

Chapter 11: Holiday Extravaganza: Festive Cheesecake Pudding Creations

Section 11.1: Pumpkin Spice Cheesecake Pudding (Thanksgiving)

Embrace the flavors of autumn with this Pumpkin Spice Cheesecake Pudding, a perfect addition to your Thanksgiving feast. This creamy and spiced dessert captures the essence of the season, filling your taste buds with warmth and nostalgia.

Ingredients:

- 8 ounces (225g) cream cheese, softened
- 1/2 cup (100g) granulated sugar
- 1 cup canned pumpkin puree
- 2 cups (480ml) heavy cream
- 1 teaspoon pumpkin pie spice
- Whipped cream, for garnish (optional)
- Cinnamon, for garnish (optional)

Instructions:

1. In a mixing bowl, beat the cream cheese and sugar together until smooth and creamy.
2. Add the pumpkin puree and pumpkin pie spice to the cream cheese mixture and beat until well combined.
3. In a separate mixing bowl, whip the heavy cream until soft peaks form.
4. Gently fold the whipped cream into the pumpkin cream cheese mixture until well combined.
5. Spoon the pumpkin spice cheesecake pudding into individual serving dishes or a large serving bowl.

6. Refrigerate for at least 2 hours to allow the pudding to set and the flavors to meld together.

7. Before serving, garnish with a dollop of whipped cream and a sprinkle of cinnamon, if desired. Celebrate Thanksgiving with the warm and comforting flavors of this pumpkin spice cheesecake pudding.

Section 11.2: Peppermint Bark Cheesecake Pudding (Christmas)

Add a touch of holiday magic to your dessert table with this Peppermint Bark Cheesecake Pudding. This festive treat combines the creaminess of cheesecake pudding with the irresistible combination of chocolate and peppermint, creating a delightful and indulgent dessert that's perfect for Christmas celebrations.

Ingredients:

- 8 ounces (225g) cream cheese, softened
- 1/2 cup (100g) powdered sugar
- 2 cups (480ml) heavy cream
- 1 teaspoon vanilla extract
- 1 cup crushed peppermint candies or candy canes
- 1/4 cup chocolate chips, melted
- Whipped cream, for garnish (optional)
- Peppermint candy pieces, for garnish (optional)

Instructions:

1. In a mixing bowl, beat the cream cheese and powdered sugar together until smooth and creamy.
2. In a separate mixing bowl, whip the heavy cream and vanilla extract until soft peaks form.
3. Gently fold the whipped cream into the cream cheese mixture until well combined.
4. Stir in the crushed peppermint candies or candy canes, reserving some for garnish if desired.
5. Spoon the peppermint bark cheesecake pudding into individual serving dishes or a large serving bowl.
6. Refrigerate for at least 2 hours to allow the pudding to set and

the flavors to meld together.

7. Before serving, drizzle melted chocolate over the pudding and garnish with whipped cream and peppermint candy pieces, if desired. Delight in the festive flavors of this peppermint bark cheesecake pudding during your Christmas celebrations.

Section 11.3: Red, White, and Blue Cheesecake Pudding (Fourth of July)

Celebrate Independence Day with the vibrant and patriotic colors of Red, White, and Blue Cheesecake Pudding. This delightful dessert layers creamy cheesecake pudding with fresh berries, creating a visually stunning and delicious treat for your Fourth of July festivities.

Ingredients:

- 8 ounces (225g) cream cheese, softened
- 1/2 cup (100g) granulated sugar
- 2 cups (480ml) heavy cream
- 1 teaspoon vanilla extract
- Fresh strawberries, sliced
- Fresh blueberries
- Whipped cream, for garnish (optional)

Instructions:

1. In a mixing bowl, beat the cream cheese and sugar together until smooth and creamy.
2. In a separate mixing bowl, whip the heavy cream and vanilla extract until soft peaks form.
3. Gently fold the whipped cream into the cream cheese mixture until well combined.
4. In individual serving glasses or bowls, layer the cheesecake pudding with fresh strawberry slices and blueberries, alternating the layers to create a red, white, and blue effect.
5. Repeat the layering process for each serving.
6. Refrigerate for at least 2 hours to allow the pudding to set and the flavors to meld together.
7. Before serving, garnish with a dollop of whipped cream and

additional fresh berries, if desired. Enjoy the patriotic spirit with each spoonful of this red, white, and blue cheesecake pudding.

Celebrate the holiday season with these festive cheesecake pudding creations. Whether you're enjoying the warm flavors of pumpkin spice on Thanksgiving, the delightful combination of peppermint and chocolate during Christmas, or the patriotic red, white, and blue dessert on the Fourth of July, these desserts will add a special touch to your holiday celebrations.

Chapter 12: Cheesecake Pudding for Breakfast: Brunch-Inspired Delights

Section 12.1: Blueberry Almond Cheesecake Pudding Parfait

Elevate your breakfast or brunch with this Blueberry Almond Cheesecake Pudding Parfait. Layers of creamy cheesecake pudding, fresh blueberries, and crunchy almonds create a delightful and satisfying morning treat that's both indulgent and nutritious.

Ingredients:

- 8 ounces (225g) cream cheese, softened
- 1/2 cup (100g) granulated sugar
- 2 cups (480ml) Greek yogurt
- 1 teaspoon vanilla extract
- Fresh blueberries
- Sliced almonds
- Honey, for drizzling (optional)

Instructions:

1. In a mixing bowl, beat the cream cheese and sugar together until smooth and creamy.
2. Add the Greek yogurt and vanilla extract to the cream cheese mixture and beat until well combined.
3. In a glass or bowl, layer the cheesecake pudding, fresh blueberries, and sliced almonds.
4. Repeat the layering process until all ingredients are used, ending with a layer of pudding on top.
5. Drizzle honey over the top layer, if desired.
6. Enjoy this delicious and protein-packed blueberry almond

cheesecake pudding parfait as a delightful start to your morning or as a brunch-inspired treat.

Section 12.2: Maple Walnut Cheesecake Pudding Bowl

Experience the comforting flavors of fall with this Maple Walnut Cheesecake Pudding Bowl. The combination of creamy cheesecake pudding, rich maple syrup, and crunchy walnuts will make your breakfast or brunch extra special.

Ingredients:

- 8 ounces (225g) cream cheese, softened
- 1/2 cup (100g) granulated sugar
- 1 cup plain Greek yogurt
- 1/4 cup maple syrup
- 1/4 teaspoon maple extract (optional)
- Chopped walnuts
- Ground cinnamon, for sprinkling

Instructions:

1. In a mixing bowl, beat the cream cheese and sugar together until smooth and creamy.
2. Add the Greek yogurt, maple syrup, and maple extract (if using) to the cream cheese mixture and beat until well combined.
3. Spoon the maple walnut cheesecake pudding into a bowl.
4. Sprinkle with chopped walnuts and a dash of ground cinnamon.
5. Enjoy this comforting and flavorful maple walnut cheesecake pudding bowl as a delightful breakfast or brunch option.

Section 12.3: Raspberry Coconut Cheesecake Pudding Smoothie

Combine the flavors of a creamy cheesecake pudding and a refreshing smoothie in this Raspberry Coconut Cheesecake Pudding Smoothie. Packed with fruity goodness and a hint of tropical coconut, this smoothie will energize your mornings and make your brunch extra satisfying.

Ingredients:

- 8 ounces (225g) cream cheese, softened
- 1/2 cup (100g) granulated sugar
- 1 cup frozen raspberries
- 1/2 cup coconut milk
- 1/4 cup plain Greek yogurt
- Shredded coconut, for garnish

Instructions:

1. In a mixing bowl, beat the cream cheese and sugar together until smooth and creamy.
2. Add the frozen raspberries, coconut milk, and Greek yogurt to the cream cheese mixture and blend until smooth and well combined.
3. Pour the raspberry coconut cheesecake pudding smoothie into a glass.
4. Garnish with shredded coconut.
5. Sip on this refreshing and satisfying raspberry coconut cheesecake pudding smoothie for a delightful breakfast or brunch experience.

Start your day with a touch of indulgence by trying these brunch-inspired cheesecake pudding delights. Whether you opt for the fruity and nutty combination of blueberries and almonds, the comforting flavors of maple and walnuts, or the refreshing fusion of raspberries and coconut, these breakfast treats will make your mornings extra special.

Chapter 13: Light and Healthy: Guilt-Free Cheesecake Pudding Alternatives

Section 13.1: Greek Yogurt Cheesecake Pudding

Indulge in a lighter and healthier version of cheesecake pudding with this Greek Yogurt Cheesecake Pudding. By incorporating protein-packed Greek yogurt, you can enjoy the creamy goodness while reducing the calories and adding a tangy twist to the classic dessert.

Ingredients:

- 1 cup plain Greek yogurt
- 4 ounces (113g) reduced-fat cream cheese, softened
- 2 tablespoons honey or maple syrup
- 1 teaspoon vanilla extract
- Fresh berries, for topping (optional)
- Mint leaves, for garnish (optional)

Instructions:

1. In a mixing bowl, combine the Greek yogurt, reduced-fat cream cheese, honey or maple syrup, and vanilla extract. Mix well until smooth and creamy.
2. Spoon the Greek yogurt cheesecake pudding into individual serving dishes.
3. Refrigerate for at least 1 hour to allow the flavors to meld together and the pudding to set.
4. Before serving, top with fresh berries and garnish with mint leaves, if desired. Enjoy this guilt-free Greek yogurt cheesecake pudding as a light and refreshing dessert option.

Section 13.2: Vegan Cheesecake Pudding with Cashews

For a dairy-free and vegan alternative, try this Vegan Cheesecake Pudding made with cashews. Cashews provide a creamy texture and richness, while keeping the recipe free from animal products. It's a perfect choice for those following a plant-based lifestyle.

Ingredients:

- 1 cup raw cashews, soaked overnight and drained
- 1/2 cup coconut milk
- 2 tablespoons lemon juice
- 3 tablespoons maple syrup or agave nectar
- 1 teaspoon vanilla extract
- Fresh fruit, for topping (optional)
- Chopped nuts, for garnish (optional)

Instructions:

1. In a blender or food processor, combine the soaked and drained cashews, coconut milk, lemon juice, maple syrup or agave nectar, and vanilla extract. Blend until smooth and creamy.
2. Spoon the vegan cheesecake pudding into individual serving dishes.
3. Refrigerate for at least 2 hours to allow the flavors to meld together and the pudding to set.
4. Before serving, top with fresh fruit and garnish with chopped nuts, if desired. Enjoy this vegan cashew cheesecake pudding as a guilt-free and plant-based dessert option.

Section 13.3: Sugar-Free Cheesecake Pudding with Stevia

If you're looking to reduce your sugar intake, this Sugar-Free Cheesecake Pudding with Stevia is the perfect choice. By using the natural sweetener stevia, you can enjoy the delightful flavors of cheesecake pudding without the added sugar, making it a guilt-free option for those watching their sugar consumption.

Ingredients:

- 8 ounces (225g) reduced-fat cream cheese, softened
- 1 cup unsweetened almond milk or coconut milk
- 1 teaspoon vanilla extract
- 1/4 teaspoon stevia powder or liquid stevia (adjust to taste)
- Fresh fruit, for topping (optional)
- Cacao nibs or shredded coconut, for garnish (optional)

Instructions:

1. In a mixing bowl, beat the reduced-fat cream cheese until smooth and creamy.
2. Add the unsweetened almond milk or coconut milk, vanilla extract, and stevia. Mix well until combined and the mixture is smooth.
3. Spoon the sugar-free cheesecake pudding into individual serving dishes.
4. Refrigerate for at least 2 hours to allow the flavors to meld together and the pudding to set.
5. Before serving, top with fresh fruit and garnish with cacao nibs or shredded coconut, if desired. Enjoy this guilt-free and sugar-free cheesecake pudding as a light and satisfying dessert option.

Satisfy your cravings for cheesecake pudding while keeping it light and healthy with these guilt-free alternatives. Whether you choose the tangy Greek yogurt variation, the creamy vegan option with cashews, or the sugar-free version sweetened with stevia, these alternatives provide a delightful and lighter twist to the classic dessert.

Chapter 14: Creamy Combinations: Cheesecake Pudding Pairings and Toppings

Section 14.1: Graham Cracker Crumble

Add a delightful crunch to your cheesecake pudding with a Graham Cracker Crumble topping. The combination of the creamy pudding and the sweet, buttery crumble creates a textural contrast that will elevate your dessert experience.

Ingredients:

- Graham crackers, crushed
- Unsalted butter, melted
- Sugar (optional)

Instructions:

1. In a bowl, combine crushed graham crackers, melted unsalted butter, and sugar (if desired). Mix well until the mixture resembles coarse crumbs.
2. Sprinkle the graham cracker crumble over your cheesecake pudding just before serving.
3. Enjoy the creamy and crunchy sensation of the cheesecake pudding paired with the delectable graham cracker crumble.

Section 14.2: Fresh Berry Compote

Enhance the fruity flavors of your cheesecake pudding with a luscious Fresh Berry Compote. The burst of tangy and sweet flavors from the berries will complement the creamy pudding perfectly, creating a harmonious and delightful combination.

Ingredients:

- Assorted fresh berries (such as strawberries, blueberries, raspberries)
- Sugar (optional)
- Lemon juice (optional)

Instructions:

1. In a saucepan, combine the fresh berries, sugar (if desired), and a squeeze of lemon juice (if desired).
2. Cook the mixture over medium heat, stirring occasionally, until the berries break down and release their juices, creating a thick and syrupy compote.
3. Remove from heat and let the compote cool to room temperature.
4. Spoon the fresh berry compote over your cheesecake pudding just before serving.
5. Experience the creamy and fruity harmony of the cheesecake pudding paired with the vibrant and tangy flavors of the fresh berry compote.

Section 14.3: Toasted Almond Slices

Add a nutty and toasty element to your cheesecake pudding with Toasted Almond Slices. The delicate crunch and rich flavor of the almonds will complement the creamy pudding, creating a delightful contrast of textures and flavors.

Ingredients:

- Almonds, sliced
- Unsalted butter

Instructions:

1. In a skillet, melt a small amount of unsalted butter over medium heat.
2. Add the sliced almonds to the skillet and toast them until golden brown, stirring occasionally to ensure even browning.
3. Remove the toasted almond slices from the heat and let them cool.
4. Sprinkle the toasted almond slices over your cheesecake pudding just before serving.
5. Enjoy the creamy and luscious cheesecake pudding paired with the nutty and toasted notes of the almond slices.

Experiment with different combinations and toppings to find your favorite creamy pairings. Whether you prefer the sweet and buttery crunch of a graham cracker crumble, the vibrant and tangy flavors of a fresh berry compote, or the nutty and toasty essence of toasted almond slices, these additions will elevate your cheesecake pudding to new heights of deliciousness.

Chapter 15: Cheesecake Pudding for Kids: Fun and Wholesome Treats

Section 15.1: Mini Cheesecake Pudding Cups with Cookie Crust

Create a playful and kid-friendly dessert with Mini Cheesecake Pudding Cups with Cookie Crust. These individual servings combine a creamy cheesecake pudding with a crunchy cookie crust, making them a delightful treat that kids will love.

Ingredients:

- Miniature cookies (such as vanilla wafers or animal-shaped cookies)
- 8 ounces (225g) cream cheese, softened
- 1/2 cup (100g) granulated sugar
- 1 cup whipped topping or whipped cream
- Assorted colorful sprinkles, for garnish (optional)

Instructions:

1. Place a mini cookie at the bottom of each serving cup or jar to create the cookie crust.
2. In a mixing bowl, beat the cream cheese and sugar together until smooth and creamy.
3. Gently fold in the whipped topping or whipped cream until well combined.
4. Spoon the cheesecake pudding mixture into the serving cups, on top of the cookie crust.
5. Garnish with colorful sprinkles, if desired.
6. Refrigerate for at least 1 hour to allow the pudding to set and the flavors to meld together.

7. Serve these mini cheesecake pudding cups as a fun and wholesome treat for kids.

Section 15.2: Cheesecake Pudding Parfait with Fresh Fruit

Introduce your kids to the goodness of fresh fruit with a Cheesecake Pudding Parfait. Layered with creamy cheesecake pudding and colorful fresh fruit, this dessert not only looks visually appealing but also provides essential vitamins and minerals for growing kids.

Ingredients:

- 8 ounces (225g) cream cheese, softened
- 1/2 cup (100g) granulated sugar
- 2 cups (480ml) whipped topping or whipped cream
- Assorted fresh fruits (such as strawberries, bananas, grapes, kiwi), sliced or diced
- Colorful cereal or granola, for garnish (optional)

Instructions:

1. In a mixing bowl, beat the cream cheese and sugar together until smooth and creamy.
2. Gently fold in the whipped topping or whipped cream until well combined.
3. In individual serving glasses or bowls, layer the cheesecake pudding and fresh fruits, alternating the layers to create a visually appealing parfait.
4. Repeat the layering process for each serving.
5. Garnish with colorful cereal or granola, if desired.
6. Refrigerate for at least 1 hour to allow the pudding to set and the flavors to meld together.
7. Serve this wholesome and fruity cheesecake pudding parfait as a delightful treat for kids.

Section 15.3: Cheesecake Pudding Smoothie

Transform cheesecake pudding into a fun and refreshing drink with a Cheesecake Pudding Smoothie. This creamy and nutritious beverage will entice your kids with its delightful flavors and make a great addition to their snack time or breakfast routine.

Ingredients:

- 8 ounces (225g) cream cheese, softened
- 1/2 cup (100g) granulated sugar
- 1 cup milk
- 1 cup frozen berries (such as strawberries, blueberries, raspberries)
- 1 ripe banana
- Whipped cream or yogurt, for topping (optional)

Instructions:

1. In a blender, combine the cream cheese, sugar, milk, frozen berries, and ripe banana. Blend until smooth and well combined.
2. Pour the cheesecake pudding smoothie into individual serving glasses.
3. Top with a dollop of whipped cream or yogurt, if desired.
4. Serve this fun and wholesome cheesecake pudding smoothie to your kids as a tasty and nourishing treat.

Make dessert time extra special for your little ones with these fun and wholesome cheesecake pudding treats. Whether you choose the mini cups with cookie crust, the layered parfait with fresh fruit, or the creamy smoothie, these kid-friendly delights will bring smiles to their faces while providing them with nutritious goodness.

Chapter 16: Gluten-Free and Vegan Cheesecake Pudding Recipes

Section 16.1: Almond Flour Crust Cheesecake Pudding Cups

Enjoy a gluten-free twist on classic cheesecake pudding with Almond Flour Crust Cheesecake Pudding Cups. These individual desserts feature a buttery almond flour crust, providing a delicious gluten-free base for the creamy cheesecake pudding.

Ingredients:

For the crust:

- 1 1/2 cups almond flour
- 3 tablespoons coconut oil, melted
- 3 tablespoons maple syrup or agave nectar
- 1/2 teaspoon vanilla extract
- Pinch of salt

For the cheesecake pudding:

- 8 ounces (225g) dairy-free cream cheese, softened
- 1/2 cup (120ml) canned coconut milk
- 1/4 cup (60ml) maple syrup or agave nectar
- 1 teaspoon lemon juice
- 1 teaspoon vanilla extract

Instructions:

1. Preheat the oven to 350°F (175°C).
2. In a bowl, combine the almond flour, melted coconut oil, maple syrup or agave nectar, vanilla extract, and a pinch of salt. Mix until well combined and the mixture resembles a crumbly

dough.

3. Divide the crust mixture among individual cupcake liners or small ramekins. Press the mixture firmly into the bottom to form the crust.

4. Bake the crusts in the preheated oven for 10 minutes, or until golden brown. Remove from the oven and let cool completely.

5. In a mixing bowl, beat the dairy-free cream cheese, coconut milk, maple syrup or agave nectar, lemon juice, and vanilla extract until smooth and creamy.

6. Spoon the cheesecake pudding mixture onto the cooled crusts.

7. Refrigerate for at least 2 hours, or until the pudding is set.

8. Serve these delightful almond flour crust cheesecake pudding cups as a gluten-free and vegan dessert option.

Section 16.2: Coconut Milk Cheesecake Pudding

Indulge in a vegan and gluten-free cheesecake pudding made with creamy coconut milk. This Coconut Milk Cheesecake Pudding provides a rich and velvety texture, perfect for those with dietary restrictions.

Ingredients:

- 8 ounces (225g) dairy-free cream cheese, softened
- 1/2 cup (120ml) canned coconut milk
- 1/4 cup (60ml) maple syrup or agave nectar
- 1 teaspoon lemon juice
- 1 teaspoon vanilla extract

Instructions:

1. In a mixing bowl, beat the dairy-free cream cheese until smooth and creamy.
2. Add the coconut milk, maple syrup or agave nectar, lemon juice, and vanilla extract. Mix well until all the ingredients are fully incorporated.
3. Spoon the coconut milk cheesecake pudding into individual serving dishes or ramekins.
4. Refrigerate for at least 2 hours, or until the pudding is set.
5. Serve this velvety and gluten-free coconut milk cheesecake pudding as a delightful vegan dessert option.

Section 16.3: Cashew-Based Cheesecake Pudding

Experience the creamy and luscious texture of cashews in this gluten-free and vegan Cashew-Based Cheesecake Pudding. Cashews provide a fantastic base for creating a dairy-free and delicious dessert.

Ingredients:

- 1 1/2 cups raw cashews, soaked overnight and drained
- 1/4 cup (60ml) coconut oil, melted
- 1/4 cup (60ml) maple syrup or agave nectar
- 1/4 cup (60ml) lemon juice
- 1/2 cup (120ml) canned coconut milk
- 1 teaspoon vanilla extract

Instructions:

1. In a blender or food processor, blend the soaked and drained cashews, melted coconut oil, maple syrup or agave nectar, lemon juice, coconut milk, and vanilla extract until smooth and creamy.
2. Spoon the cashew-based cheesecake pudding into individual serving dishes or ramekins.
3. Refrigerate for at least 2 hours, or until the pudding is set.
4. Enjoy this creamy and gluten-free cashew-based cheesecake pudding as a delectable vegan dessert option.

Indulge in the rich and creamy flavors of cheesecake pudding even if you follow a gluten-free and vegan lifestyle. Whether you opt for the almond flour crust cups, the coconut milk-based pudding, or the cashew-based variation, these recipes offer delicious alternatives that will satisfy your cravings without compromising your dietary preferences.

Chapter 17: Boozy and Bold: Cheesecake Pudding with Alcohol Infusions

Section 17.1: Baileys Irish Cream Cheesecake Pudding

Infuse your cheesecake pudding with the rich and creamy flavors of Baileys Irish Cream. This Boozy Baileys Irish Cream Cheesecake Pudding offers a decadent twist that will please the adults in the room.

Ingredients:

- 8 ounces (225g) cream cheese, softened
- 1/2 cup (100g) granulated sugar
- 2 tablespoons Baileys Irish Cream liqueur
- 1 teaspoon vanilla extract
- Whipped cream, for garnish (optional)
- Chocolate shavings, for garnish (optional)

Instructions:

1. In a mixing bowl, beat the cream cheese and sugar together until smooth and creamy.
2. Add the Baileys Irish Cream liqueur and vanilla extract to the cream cheese mixture and beat until well combined.
3. Spoon the Baileys Irish Cream cheesecake pudding into individual serving dishes.
4. Refrigerate for at least 2 hours to allow the pudding to set and the flavors to meld together.
5. Before serving, garnish with a dollop of whipped cream and a sprinkle of chocolate shavings, if desired. Enjoy the indulgent and boozy flavors of this Baileys Irish Cream cheesecake pudding.

Section 17.2: Amaretto Infused Cheesecake Pudding

Add a touch of nutty sophistication to your cheesecake pudding with Amaretto liqueur. This Amaretto Infused Cheesecake Pudding offers a unique flavor profile that will entice your taste buds.

Ingredients:

- 8 ounces (225g) cream cheese, softened
- 1/2 cup (100g) granulated sugar
- 2 tablespoons Amaretto liqueur
- 1 teaspoon almond extract
- Sliced almonds, for garnish (optional)
- Fresh berries, for garnish (optional)

Instructions:

1. In a mixing bowl, beat the cream cheese and sugar together until smooth and creamy.
2. Add the Amaretto liqueur and almond extract to the cream cheese mixture and beat until well combined.
3. Spoon the Amaretto-infused cheesecake pudding into individual serving dishes.
4. Refrigerate for at least 2 hours to allow the pudding to set and the flavors to meld together.
5. Before serving, garnish with sliced almonds and fresh berries, if desired. Indulge in the nutty and bold flavors of this Amaretto-infused cheesecake pudding.

Section 17.3: Rum Raisin Cheesecake Pudding

Transport your taste buds to the tropics with the tantalizing combination of rum and raisins in this Rum Raisin Cheesecake Pudding. The boozy kick and plump raisins make this dessert a grown-up delight.

Ingredients:

- 8 ounces (225g) cream cheese, softened
- 1/2 cup (100g) granulated sugar
- 2 tablespoons dark rum
- 1/2 cup raisins
- Whipped cream, for garnish (optional)
- Ground cinnamon, for garnish (optional)

Instructions:

1. In a small bowl, soak the raisins in the dark rum for at least 1 hour to allow them to plump up and absorb the flavors.
2. In a mixing bowl, beat the cream cheese and sugar together until smooth and creamy.
3. Drain the soaked raisins and add them to the cream cheese mixture. Beat until well combined.
4. Spoon the rum raisin cheesecake pudding into individual serving dishes.
5. Refrigerate for at least 2 hours to allow the pudding to set and the flavors to meld together.
6. Before serving, garnish with a dollop of whipped cream and a sprinkle of ground cinnamon, if desired. Enjoy the bold and boozy flavors of this rum raisin cheesecake pudding.

Add a touch of sophistication and indulgence to your cheesecake pudding with these boozy and bold flavors. Whether you choose the creamy and rich Baileys Irish Cream variation, the nutty elegance of Amaretto, or the tropical kick of rum and raisins, these alcohol-infused cheesecake pudding recipes will impress your guests and leave them craving more.

Chapter 18: Chilled Delights: Cheesecake Pudding Frozen Desserts
Section 18.1: Cheesecake Pudding Ice Cream

Beat the heat with a luscious and creamy Cheesecake Pudding Ice Cream. This frozen delight combines the flavors of cheesecake pudding with the smooth and velvety texture of ice cream, creating the perfect treat for a hot summer day.

Ingredients:

- 8 ounces (225g) cream cheese, softened
- 1/2 cup (100g) granulated sugar
- 2 cups (480ml) heavy cream
- 1 teaspoon vanilla extract
- Graham cracker crumbs, for topping (optional)

Instructions:

1. In a mixing bowl, beat the cream cheese and sugar together until smooth and creamy.
2. In a separate mixing bowl, whip the heavy cream and vanilla extract until soft peaks form.
3. Gently fold the whipped cream into the cream cheese mixture until well combined.
4. Transfer the mixture into an ice cream maker and churn according to the manufacturer's instructions.
5. Once churned, transfer the ice cream to a lidded container and freeze for at least 4 hours, or until firm.
6. Serve the cheesecake pudding ice cream in bowls or cones,

and sprinkle with graham cracker crumbs for an extra touch of texture and flavor.

Section 18.2: Frozen Cheesecake Pudding Bars

Enjoy the convenience of handheld frozen treats with Frozen Cheesecake Pudding Bars. These creamy and chilled bars are perfect for satisfying your cheesecake cravings on a hot summer day.

Ingredients:

- 8 ounces (225g) cream cheese, softened
- 1/2 cup (100g) granulated sugar
- 2 cups (480ml) whipped topping or whipped cream
- Graham cracker crust (store-bought or homemade)
- Fresh berries, for garnish (optional)

Instructions:

1. In a mixing bowl, beat the cream cheese and sugar together until smooth and creamy.
2. Gently fold in the whipped topping or whipped cream until well combined.
3. Spread the cheesecake pudding mixture evenly over a prepared graham cracker crust in a baking dish or lined baking pan.
4. Freeze the mixture for at least 4 hours, or until firm.
5. Once frozen, cut the mixture into bars or squares.
6. Garnish with fresh berries, if desired, before serving. Enjoy these refreshing and creamy frozen cheesecake pudding bars.

Section 18.3: Cheesecake Pudding Popsicles

Cool down with Cheesecake Pudding Popsicles, the perfect frozen treat for both kids and adults. These popsicles capture the creamy and indulgent flavors of cheesecake pudding in a refreshing and portable form.

Ingredients:

- 8 ounces (225g) cream cheese, softened
- 1/2 cup (100g) granulated sugar
- 1 cup milk
- 1 teaspoon vanilla extract
- Assorted fresh fruits or crushed cookies (optional)

Instructions:

1. In a mixing bowl, beat the cream cheese and sugar together until smooth and creamy.
2. Add the milk and vanilla extract to the cream cheese mixture and beat until well combined.
3. Pour the cheesecake pudding mixture into popsicle molds.
4. If desired, add chunks of fresh fruits or crushed cookies to the molds for added texture and flavor.
5. Insert popsicle sticks into the molds and freeze for at least 4 hours, or until completely frozen.
6. Run the molds under warm water to release the popsicles, and enjoy these delightful and frosty cheesecake pudding popsicles.

Cool off and satisfy your sweet tooth with these refreshing frozen cheesecake pudding treats. Whether you choose the velvety cheesecake pudding ice cream, the convenient and handheld frozen bars, or the delightful cheesecake pudding popsicles, these chilled delights will keep you cool and satisfied during the hot summer months.

Chapter 19: Artful Presentation: Decorating and Garnishing Cheesecake Pudding

Section 19.1: Whipped Cream and Fresh Fruit Swirls

Create a visually appealing presentation for your cheesecake pudding by adding Whipped Cream and Fresh Fruit Swirls. These elegant and artistic decorations will make your dessert stand out and tempt your taste buds.

Instructions:

1. Prepare your cheesecake pudding according to the recipe of your choice.
2. Fill a piping bag fitted with a star tip with whipped cream.
3. Pipe a dollop of whipped cream onto the center of the pudding.
4. Using a toothpick or skewer, gently swirl the whipped cream in a circular motion to create a decorative pattern.
5. Garnish the swirls with fresh fruit slices or berries, placing them strategically around the whipped cream design.
6. Repeat the process for each serving of cheesecake pudding, creating unique and eye-catching presentations.

Section 19.2: Chocolate Ganache Drizzle

Add a touch of decadence to your cheesecake pudding with a Chocolate Ganache Drizzle. The rich and glossy chocolate will create a stunning contrast against the creamy pudding, making your dessert even more enticing.

Instructions:

1. Prepare your cheesecake pudding according to the recipe of your choice.
2. In a small saucepan, heat equal parts of heavy cream and chocolate chips over low heat, stirring continuously until the chocolate has melted and the mixture is smooth and shiny.
3. Let the chocolate ganache cool slightly until it thickens to a drizzling consistency.
4. Drizzle the chocolate ganache over the top of the cheesecake pudding in a zigzag pattern or any desired design.
5. Allow the ganache to set for a few minutes before serving, or refrigerate briefly for a firmer ganache finish.

Section 19.3: Cookie Crumbs and Sprinkles

Enhance the texture and visual appeal of your cheesecake pudding by sprinkling it with Cookie Crumbs and Sprinkles. These simple yet effective garnishes will add a pop of color and a delightful crunch to your dessert.

Instructions:

1. Prepare your cheesecake pudding according to the recipe of your choice.
2. Crush your favorite cookies, such as graham crackers or chocolate sandwich cookies, to create fine crumbs.
3. Sprinkle the cookie crumbs generously over the top of the pudding, creating an even layer.
4. Sprinkle colorful sprinkles over the cookie crumbs, allowing them to cascade down the sides of the pudding.
5. Gently press the crumbs and sprinkles into the pudding to ensure they adhere.
6. Serve your beautifully garnished cheesecake pudding and delight in the combination of flavors, textures, and aesthetics.

Section 19.4: Mint Leaves and Chocolate Shavings

Add an elegant and refreshing touch to your cheesecake pudding with Mint Leaves and Chocolate Shavings. The vibrant green mint leaves and delicate chocolate curls will create a sophisticated presentation that will impress your guests.

Instructions:

1. Prepare your cheesecake pudding according to the recipe of your choice.
2. Wash and dry fresh mint leaves, ensuring they are free from any moisture.
3. Place a few mint leaves on top of the pudding, arranging them artistically or in a circular pattern.
4. Using a vegetable peeler or a dedicated chocolate shaver, gently shave curls of chocolate onto the pudding.
5. Scatter the chocolate shavings around the mint leaves, creating a visually appealing contrast.
6. Serve your beautifully decorated cheesecake pudding and enjoy the combination of flavors and aesthetics.

Elevate the presentation of your cheesecake pudding by incorporating these decorative ideas. Whether you opt for the elegance of whipped cream and fresh fruit swirls, the richness of a chocolate ganache drizzle, the crunch of cookie crumbs and sprinkles, or the sophistication of mint leaves and chocolate shavings, these artful decorations will make your dessert a feast for the eyes as well as the taste buds.

Chapter 20: Cheesecake Pudding Masterclass: Advanced Techniques and Tips

Section 20.1: Achieving a Silky Smooth Texture

One of the hallmarks of a perfect cheesecake pudding is a silky-smooth texture. To achieve this, follow these tips:

Ensure the cream cheese is softened: Make sure your cream cheese is at room temperature before mixing it with other ingredients. Softened cream cheese blends more easily, resulting in a smoother texture.

Use a high-quality blender or food processor: A powerful blender or food processor will help achieve a velvety texture by thoroughly blending all the ingredients together.

Strain the mixture: To eliminate any lumps or inconsistencies, pass the cheesecake pudding mixture through a fine-mesh strainer. This step ensures a silky smooth result.

Section 20.2: Perfecting the Creaminess

The creaminess of cheesecake pudding is what makes it truly indulgent. Here are some tips to achieve the perfect creamy consistency:

Beat the cream cheese thoroughly: Take the time to beat the cream cheese until it becomes smooth and fluffy. This step ensures a creamy base for your pudding.

Incorporate whipped topping or whipped cream: Adding whipped topping or whipped cream to the mixture lightens the texture and enhances the creaminess. Gently fold it in until fully incorporated.

Use full-fat ingredients: opt for full-fat cream cheese, whole milk, and heavy cream to achieve a rich and creamy texture. The higher fat content contributes to a luxurious mouthfeel.

Section 20.3: Preventing Cracking

Cracking can sometimes occur on the surface of cheesecake pudding. Follow these tips to prevent cracks:

Avoid overmixing: Overmixing can introduce excess air into the mixture, leading to cracks during baking or setting. Mix the ingredients until just combined.

Use a water bath: Place the baking dish or ramekins containing the cheesecake pudding in a larger pan filled with hot water before baking. The water bath creates a moist environment, preventing the pudding from drying out and cracking.

Allow gradual cooling: After baking or chilling, allow the cheesecake pudding to cool gradually. Sudden temperature changes can cause cracks. Start by cooling it at room temperature for a while before transferring it to the refrigerator.

Section 20.4: Experimenting with Flavors and Additions

Cheesecake pudding provides a canvas for endless flavor variations. Here are some ideas to get creative with your flavors:

Infuse flavors: Add extracts, such as almond, lemon, or coconut, to the cream cheese mixture to infuse it with delicious flavors.

Incorporate mix-ins: Fold in crushed cookies, chocolate chips, fruit purees, or nuts to add texture and flavor bursts to your cheesecake pudding.

Create unique crusts: Experiment with different crust options, such as graham cracker crusts, cookie crusts, or nut-based crusts, to complement your chosen flavors.

Pair with complementary sauces: Serve your cheesecake pudding with a drizzle of caramel sauce, fruit compote, or chocolate ganache to enhance the overall flavor profile.

Section 20.5: Serving and Storage Tips

To ensure the best experience with your cheesecake pudding, consider the following serving and storage tips:

Serve chilled: Cheesecake pudding is best enjoyed chilled. Allow it to set in the refrigerator for the recommended time to achieve the desired consistency and flavor.

Garnish just before serving: For optimal presentation, add decorative elements, such as whipped cream, fresh fruit, or chocolate shavings, just before serving to maintain their freshness and appeal.

Store properly: Store any leftover cheesecake pudding in an airtight container in the refrigerator. Consume within a few days to maintain the best flavor and texture.

Freezing considerations: While cheesecake pudding can be frozen, it may alter the texture slightly. If freezing, wrap individual portions tightly in plastic wrap or store in a freezer-safe container. Thaw in the refrigerator before serving.

By applying these advanced techniques and tips, you'll elevate your cheesecake pudding to new heights of perfection. From achieving a silky smooth texture and perfecting the creaminess to preventing cracks and exploring flavor variations, you'll become a master of creating irresistible cheesecake pudding desserts.

In conclusion, the "Cheesecake Pudding Cookbook" offers a delectable collection of recipes and techniques to satisfy your cravings for creamy, indulgent desserts. Throughout the 20 chapters, we explored a wide range of cheesecake pudding variations, from classic favorites to innovative creations, catering to various dietary preferences and occasions.

We began by introducing the basics of cheesecake pudding, guiding you through the essential ingredients, equipment, and techniques needed to achieve a perfect result. From there, we delved into chapters dedicated to different flavor profiles, including fruity infusions, chocolate indulgence, nut-infused delights, seasonal variations, international inspirations, and guilt-free alternatives. We also explored single servings, holiday-themed creations, brunch-inspired delights, and options for kids.

To enhance your cheesecake pudding experience, we provided tips on garnishing and decorating techniques, guiding you in creating artful presentations that will impress both visually and in taste. We also covered advanced techniques and tips to elevate your cheesecake pudding mastery, ensuring a silky smooth texture, perfect creaminess, and avoiding common pitfalls such as cracking.

Throughout the cookbook, we encouraged experimentation with flavors, mix-ins, and crust options, empowering you to customize your cheesecake pudding creations to suit your preferences. We highlighted the importance of presentation, offering ideas for garnishes, sauces, and serving suggestions to make your desserts truly memorable.

Whether you're a novice in the kitchen or an experienced home cook, the "Cheesecake Pudding Cookbook" will be your guide to creating irresistible and satisfying desserts that will delight your taste buds and impress your family and friends. So, grab your apron, gather your ingredients, and let the journey to cheesecake pudding perfection begin!

www.ingramcontent.com/pod-product-compliance
Lightning Source LLC
Chambersburg PA
CBHW031343160726
47993CB00002B/813